# The Artist of This Book is

_____

# The Llama of This Book is

_____

© 2021 Ludvig & Lucy

Artwork by Creative Fabrica

# DAY 1 - DRAW YOUR LLAMA

# DAY 2 - DRAW YOUR LLAMA WITH A HAT AND SUNGLASSES

# DAY 3 - DRAW YOUR LLAMA WITH YOUR FAVORITE OUTFIT

DAY 4 - DRAW YOUR LLAMA IN THE RAIN

DAY 5 - DRAW YOUR LLAMA AS A SNOWMAN

DAY 6 - DRAW YOUR LLAMA SKIING

# DAY 7 - DRAW YOUR LLAMA IN A SNOWBALL FIGHT

# Day 8 - Draw your Llama as Santa

# Day 9 - Draw your Llama vacuuming

# DAY 10 - DRAW YOUR LLAMA DOING THE DISHES

DAY 11 - DRAW YOUR LLAMA IN THE GARDEN

# DAY 12 - DRAW YOUR LLAMA DOING LAUNDRY

# DAY 13 - DRAW YOUR LLAMA AS AN INFLUENCER

# DAY 14 - DRAW YOUR LLAMA DOING A SELFIE

DAY 15 - DRAW YOUR LLAMA AT A PARTY

# DAY 16 - DRAW YOUR LLAMA AS A DIGITAL NOMAD

# DAY 17 - DRAW YOUR LLAMA CLIMBING A MOUNTAIN

# DAY 18 - DRAW YOUR LLAMA SKYDIVING

DAY 19 - DRAW YOUR LLAMA AT A SAFARI

DAY 20 - DRAW YOUR LLAMA RIDING A JET SKI

# DAY 21 - DRAW YOUR LLAMA WATCHING TV

# Day 22 - Draw your Llama eating Pizza

# DAY 23 - DRAW YOUR LLAMA GAMING

DAY 24 - DRAW YOUR LLAMA PLAYING BOARD GAMES WITH FRIENDS

# Day 25 - Draw your Llama Doing Yoga

# DAY 26 - DRAW YOUR LLAMA PICKING FLOWERS

DAY 27 - DRAW YOUR LLAMA SLEEPING

# Day 28 - Draw your Llama meditating

# Day 29 - Draw your Llama at the Beach

# DAY 30 - DRAW YOUR LLAMA SURFING

DAY 31 - DRAW YOUR LLAMA SNORKELING

# DAY 32 - DRAW YOUR LLAMA RELAXING IN A HAMMOCK

DAY 33 - DRAW YOUR LLAMA AS A BABY

# DAY 34 - DRAW YOUR LLAMA AT THE PLAYGROUND

# DAY 35 - DRAW YOUR LLAMA PLAYING WITH TOYS

DAY 36 - DRAW YOUR LLAMA AS A PILOT

DAY 37 - DRAW YOUR LLAMA DANCING

# DAY 38 - DRAW YOUR LLAMA AT A CONCERT

# DAY 39 - DRAW YOUR LLAMA TAKING A BATH

# Day 40 - Draw your llama at the spa

Day 41 - Draw your Llama Brushing Teeth

DAY 42 - DRAW YOUR LLAMA LOOKING IN THE MIRROR

# DAY 43 - DRAW YOUR LLAMA IN LOVE

DAY 44 - DRAW YOUR LLAMA LISTENING TO MUSIC

# Day 45 - Draw your llama cooking

# DAY 46 - DRAW YOUR LLAMA DRINKING MOCKTAILS

DAY 47 - DRAW YOUR LLAMA AT COLLEGE

# Day 48 - Draw your Llama at the movie theater

# DAY 49 - DRAW A CLASS PORTRAIT PHOTO OF YOUR LLAMA

DAY 50 - DRAW YOUR LLAMA SAILING

DAY 51 - DRAW YOUR LLAMA EATING ICE CREAM

DAY 52 - DRAW YOUR LLAMA IN THE POOL

DAY 53 - DRAW YOUR LLAMA AT A SWIMMING COMPETITION

DAY 54 - DRAW YOUR LLAMA WALKING THE DOG

DAY 55 - DRAW YOUR LLAMA WITH A PET GOLDFISH

# DAY 56 - DRAW YOUR LLAMA BIRDWATCHING

DAY 57 - DRAW YOUR LLAMA PETTING THE CAT

DAY 58 - DRAW YOUR LLAMA AS A TEACHER

# DAY 59 - DRAW YOUR LLAMA AT THE OFFICE

DAY 60 - DRAW YOUR LLAMA AS A DOCTOR

DAY 61 - DRAW YOUR LLAMA AS A JUDGE

DAY 62 - DRAW YOUR LLAMA DRINKING A MILKSHAKE

# DAY 63 - DRAW YOUR LLAMA EATING A BURGER

DAY 64 - DRAW YOUR LLAMA BAKING

# DAY 65 - DRAW YOUR LLAMA PLAYING THE GUITAR

# DAY 66 - DRAW YOUR LLAMA SINGING

# DAY 67 - DRAW YOUR LLAMA PLAYING THE DRUMS

DAY 68 - DRAW YOUR LLAMA AT THE OLYMPIC GAMES

DAY 69 - DRAW YOUR LLAMA JUMPING ON THE TRAMPOLINE

DAY 70 - DRAW YOUR LLAMA AT THE GYM

DAY 71 - DRAW YOUR LLAMA RUNNING

DAY 72 - DRAW YOUR LLAMA PLAYING FOOTBALL

DAY 73 - DRAW YOUR LLAMA AS A FASHIONISTA

DAY 74 - DRAW YOUR LLAMA ON THE RUNWAY

DAY 75 - DRAW YOUR LLAMA WITH MAKE-UP

# DAY 76 - DRAW YOUR LLAMA AS A PHOTOGRAPHER

# DAY 77 - DRAW YOUR LLAMA AS A GLOBETROTTER

# DAY 78 - DRAW YOUR LLAMA EXPLORING THE BIG CITY

DAY 79 - DRAW YOUR LLAMA AT THE AIRPORT

# Day 80 - Draw your Llama Backpacking

# DAY 81 - DRAW YOUR LLAMA AT THE COFFEESHOP

DAY 82 - DRAW YOUR LLAMA EATING DONUTS

DAY 83 - DRAW YOUR LLAMA DRIVING A BICYCLE

DAY 84 - DRAW YOUR LLAMA WITH A LASSO

# DAY 85 - DRAW YOUR LLAMA MILKING A COW

Day 86 - Draw your Llama Driving a Tractor

DAY 87 - DRAW YOUR LLAMA RIDING A HORSE

# DAY 88 - DRAW YOUR LLAMA PAINTING

DAY 89 - DRAW YOUR LLAMA WRITING A BOOK

# DAY 90 - DRAW YOUR LLAMA SEWING

DAY 91 - DRAW YOUR LLAMA DRIVING A CAR

DAY 92 - DRAW YOUR LLAMA AS AN OLD LLAMA

DAY 93 - DRAW YOUR LLAMA AS A PARENT

DAY 94 - DRAW YOUR LLAMA READING

DAY 95 - DRAW YOUR LLAMA PLAYING THE PIANO

DAY 96 - DRAW YOUR LLAMA HAVING A BIRTHDAY PARTY

# DAY 97 - DRAW YOUR LLAMA KNITTING

DAY 98 - DRAW YOUR LLAMA LAUGHING

DAY 99 - DRAW YOUR LLAMA TALKING ON THE PHONE

DAY 100 - DRAW YOUR LLAMA HOW YOU LIKE

www.ingramcontent.com/pod-product-compliance
Lightning Source LLC
Chambersburg PA
CBHW080542220526
45466CB00010B/3009